starting

DATA HANDLING

starting DATA HANDLING

For National Curriculum levels 1–3

SPECTRUM MATHS

Dave Kirkby

UNWIN HYMAN

Published in 1990 by
UNWIN HYMAN LIMITED
15/17 Broadwick Street
London W1V 1FP

© Dave Kirkby 1990

The purchase of this
copyright material
confers the right on the
purchasing institution to
photocopy the pupils'
pages without any
specific authorisation by
the publisher. No other
part of this publication
may be reproduced, stored
in a retrieval system, or
transmitted in any form
or by any means,
electronic, mechanical,
photocopying, recording
or otherwise, without the
prior permission of Unwin
Hyman Limited.

British Library Cataloguing in Publication Data
Kirkby, Dave
　　Spectrum mathematics.
　　Starting data handling
　　1. Mathematics
　　I. Title　II. Series
　　510

ISBN 0 04 448198 5

Designed and illustrated by AMR, Basingstoke
Printed in Great Britain by The Alden Press Ltd, Oxford
Bound by Hunter & Foulis Ltd, Edinburgh

Contents

1	Birthmonths		21	Jungle
2	Cats and dogs		22	Cards
3	Colour		23	Shape sort
4	Absences		24	Favourite season
5	Transport to school		25	Ice cream
6	Fruits		26	Crisps
7	Hair colour		27	Left or right?
8	Post		28	Tables
9	Birds		29	Pencils
10	Our cars		30	Cartoon characters
11	Our pets		31	Comics
12	Sweets		32	Car numbers
13	Legs		33	Activities
14	Fish tank		34	Ladybirds
15	Drinks		35	Coin maps
16	Odds or evens		36	More or less
17	Linking dots		37	Down at the farm
18	Twenty coins		38	Animals
19	Clocks		39	Nine creatures
20	Three colours		40	My family and friends

Some suggested software which may be useful for 'Handling data'

Key Stage 1 and 2

Our Facts
Branch } NCET University of Warwick
Notice Board

Key Stage 2 and 3

Junior Find   RESOURCE, Exeter Road, Doncaster DN2 4PY

Grass
Grasshopper } Newman College, Garners Lane, Bartley Green, Birmingham B32 3NT

Introduction

Most schools use a mathematics scheme or schemes to teach basic skills and concepts, but teachers still require a wide range of materials to supplement these schemes. Such materials are provided by the **Spectrum Maths** series.

This is a series of three books of data handling activities primarily for the primary years, although secondary school teachers with low attaining pupils will also find these books useful.

They are defined in terms of three ability levels.

Starting Data Handling – for National Curriculum levels 1–3
More Data Handling – for National Curriculum levels 2–5
Go Further with Data Handling – for National Curriculum levels 3–6

Each book contains 40 data handling activities in the form of:

- a photocopiable pupil sheet
- detailed teacher's notes about the mathematical content and objectives, the apparatus required, activities for the pupils, and examples of questions to be asked of the pupils.

The National Curriculum in Mathematics has devoted three of its 14 Attainment Targets to Data Handling. Namely:

> AT 12: Pupils should collect, record and process data.
> AT 13: Pupils should represent and interpret data.
> AT 14: Pupils should understand estimate and calculate probabilities.

Spectrum Maths Data Handling should prove an invaluable resource for pupils and teachers in meeting the needs and requirements of the data handling elements of the National Curriculum.

Although the main focus of the material is data handling, many of the activities will naturally involve other aspects of the National Curriculum. Particularly prominent is:

AT 9: Using and applying mathematics.

The **Cockcroft Report** also emphasises the importance of data handling:

> 'Throughout the primary years attention should be paid to methods of presenting mathematical information in pictorial and graphical form, and also to interpreting information which is presented in this way. It can often be the case that graphical work lacks variety and progression, so that older children are limited to drawing graphs which differ little from those which are to be found in infant classrooms. Children need experience of a wide variety of graphical work; the mere drawing of graphs should not be over-emphasised. It is essential to discuss and interpret the information which is displayed both in graphs which children have themselves drawn and also in graphs which they have not.'
>
> [**Cockcroft Report**: *Mathematics Counts* paragraph 293]

This series does not claim to be a fully comprehensive coverage of all aspects of data handling. The format of photocopiable material accompanied by detailed teacher's notes is not appropriate, for example, for computer use.

Using the pupils' sheets

Number

The **pupil sheets** take the form of either:

a **data source,**

or **data representation.**

These are both used for providing children with experiences in the collection and analysis of data.

Using the teacher's notes

Main focus of the data handling activity

Brief outline of the mathematical content and purpose of the activity.

Apparatus

Description of any apparatus required.

Activity

Children may need to perform some activity based on the pupil sheet before they are ready for the suggested 'sample activities'. This section outlines such activities.

LEVEL	Profile Component 1				Profile Component 2		
	UA	N	A	M	UA	S	D
1							
2							
3							
4							
5							
6							
7							
8							
9							
10							

KEY UA Using and Applying Mathematics
N Number
A Algebra
M Measures
S Shape and Space
D Handling Data

The teacher's notes for each activity contain the above table. This table refers to the attainment targets and levels of the National Curriculum. An attempt has been made to locate, by means of dots in the table, the approximate content level for each activity but it must be appreciated that many activities can be performed at a variety of different levels.

Handling the data – sample activities

This section contains examples of activities for children using the pupil sheet as a starting point. It is assumed that the teacher will discuss activities with the pupils and lead them appropriately. The notes highlight particular components of data handling, namely, the ability to

collect data
record data
process data
represent data
interpret data

In some cases particular activities may embody all of these components, leading pupils towards the more general **'using and applying mathematics'**.

Interpreting the data – sample questions

It is most important that pupils are given experiences in interpreting data and its representation. This section provides some examples for the teacher of questions he/she might ask in order to provide pupils with such experiences. Pupils are given further experiences in interpreting data when asked to write sentences about specific data and its representation.

1 Birthmonths

Block graphs

Drawing a block graph representing the birthmonth for each child in the class. Interpreting the graph.

Activity

Produce a list showing the names of children in the class and their birthmonth.

LEVEL	Profile Component 1				Profile Component 2		
	UA	N	A	M	UA	S	D
1							
2							●
3							
4							
5							
6							
7							
8							
9							
10							

D2   Block graphs

Handling the data – sample activities

- Colour the blocks to build a block graph representing the class' birthmonths (**collect, represent data**).
  Write some sentences about the graph (**interpret data**).

- Draw a block graph for the birthmonths for another class (**collect, record, represent, interpret data**).

- Draw a graph to show the birthmonths of your class and another class together.

Interpreting the data – sample questions

- How many children have a birthday in March, August,...?
- How many have a birthday in the same month as you?
- How many have a birthday this month, next month, last month?
- Which months have two birthdays, three birthdays,...?
- Are there any months with no birthdays?
- How many birthdays in January or February, in June or July,...?
- Were most children born in the first half of the year?

Birthmonths

1

Birthmonths of the class

Children

7
6
5
4
3
2
1

January February March April May June July August September October November December

Month

Write some sentences about the graph.

starting **DATA HANDLING** **SPECTRUM MATHS**

2 Cats and dogs

Mapping diagrams

Block graphs

Drawing a mapping diagram to represent pets owned by a group of children. Interpreting the diagram. Drawing a block graph to show the number of each pet owned by the group.

LEVEL	Profile Component 1				Profile Component 2		
	UA	N	A	M	UA	S	D
1							●
2							●
3							
4							
5							
6							
7							
8							
9							
10							

D1 Mapping diagrams
D2 Block graphs

Activity

Pupils choose six children and write their names in the rectangles on the left. Write some types of pet in the spaces in the right e.g. cat, rabbit, dog, hamster, fish.

Handling the data – sample activities

- Draw a mapping diagram by joining names to pets owned (**represent data**).

- Draw another diagram for a different group of children (**represent data**). Write something about the diagrams (**interpret data**).

- Draw a block graph to show the number of each pet owned by the group of pupils (**represent data**).

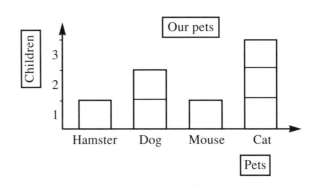

Interpreting the data – sample questions

- Which children have a pet dog, rabbit,...?
- How many children have a cat?
- What pet does ____ have ? What about ____?
- Who has more than one pet?
- Who has the most pets?
- Which is the most common pet?

3 Colour

Block graphs

Data collection

Interpreting a block graph relating to favourite colours, leading to drawing a block graph of the same.

LEVEL	Profile Component 1				Profile Component 2		
	UA	N	A	M	UA	S	D
1		●					
2							●
3							
4							
5							
6							
7							
8							
9							
10							

N1 Ordering single – digit numbers.
D2 Block graphs.

Handling the data – sample activities

- Write about one of the colours,

  e.g. RED 'It is the favourite for four children',
  'It is more popular than green',
  It has one vote more than yellow',
  (**interpret data**).

- **Collect data** on favourite colours for each member of the class. Draw a block graph to illustrate the information (**record, process, represent data**). Discuss and compare (**interpret data**).

Interpreting the data – sample questions

- How many children have a favourite colour of red, green,...?
- Which colour is the favourite for four children?
- Which is the most popular colour?
- How many more preferred red to green?
- How many votes did green have less than yellow?
- How many have a favourite colour of green or blue?
- How many children were involved altogether?

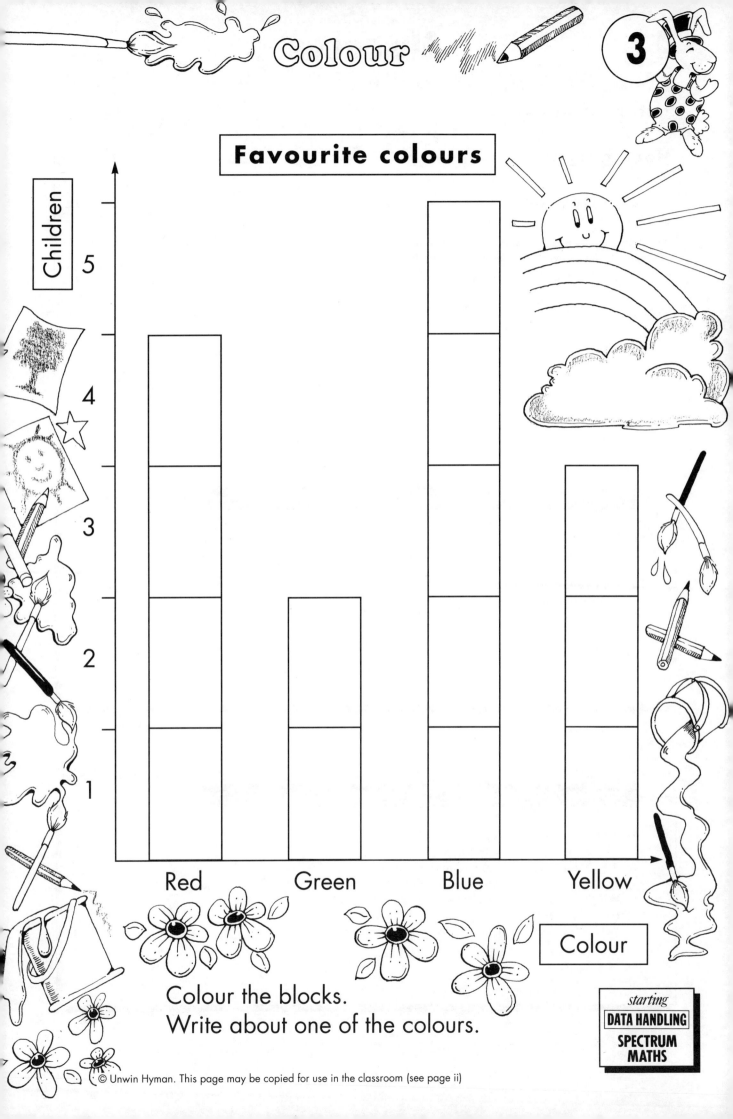

4 Absences

Picture graphs

Block graphs

Data collection

Interpreting a picture graph representing the number of absences for a class of pupils over a period of a week. Collecting data and drawing a picture graph for the class absences.

LEVEL	Profile Component 1				Profile Component 2		
	UA	N	A	M	UA	S	D
1						●	●
2						●	
3						●	
4							
5							
6							
7							
8							
9							
10							

D1 Picture graphs.
D2 Block graphs.

Handling the data – sample activities

- **Collect data** on your class absences for last week. Draw a graph to illustrate the information (**represent data**).

- **Collect data** for another class and draw a picture graph. Combine the results for both classes (**using and applying; process, represent data**).

Interpreting the data – sample questions

- How many children were absent on Monday, Tuesday,...?
- Which day had the most absentees?
- Which day had no absentees, three absentees,...?
- How many more children were absent on Thursday than Friday,...?
- Which day had the best attendance, worst attendance?
- How many absences were there over the whole week?
- Which days had more than two, less than three,... absences?

Absences

This data shows the absences in a class for one week.

Monday				
Tuesday				
Wednesday				
Thursday				
Friday				

 represents 1 child

Write some sentences about this.

starting **DATA HANDLING** **SPECTRUM MATHS**

5 Transport to School

Block graphs

Data collection

Interpreting a block graph relating to methods of transport to school. Drawing a block graph to show the class' methods of transport to school.

LEVEL	Profile Component 1				Profile Component 2		
	UA	N	A	M	UA	S	D
1					●		
2					●		●
3					●		
4							
5							
6							
7							
8							
9							
10							

D2   Block graphs.

Handling the data – sample activities

- **Collect data** on methods of transport to school for pupils in the class. Draw a block graph to illustrate the results (**represent data**). Write about it (**interpret data**).

- Collect data and draw a block graph for another class. Compare the two. (**Using and applying; record, process, represent, interpret data**).

Interpreting the data – sample questions

- How many children travelled to school by bus, car,...?
- Which method of transport is the most common, least common?
- Which method of transport is used by four children only?
- How many more children came by car than by bus?
- How many children came by car or walked?
- How many children did not walk?
- How many children altogether?
- Which means of transport is used by more than two children?

6 Fruits

Sorting

Carroll diagrams

Mapping diagrams

Block graphs

Sorting activities based on a selection of fruits.

LEVEL	Profile Component 1				Profile Component 2		
	UA	N	A	M	UA	S	D
1							●
2							●
3							
4							
5							
6							
7							
8							
9							
10							

D1 Sorting. Mapping diagrams.
D2 Carroll diagrams. Block graphs.

Activity

After discussion, the fruits can be cut out and stuck on charts to illustrate mapping diagrams, Carroll diagrams, Venn diagrams etc.

Handling the data – sample activities

- Try a variety of sorting activities by cutting out the pictures of fruits and placing them on to Carroll diagrams (**represent data**).
  Examples of sorts:
  like v **don't like**
  have eaten v **have not eaten**
  green v **not green**
  yellow v **not yellow**
  have stones v **don't have stones**
  have pips v **don't have pips**
  sweet taste v **sour taste**

Like	Don't like

- Draw mapping diagrams for favourite green fruit/yellow fruit,... (**represent data**).

- Draw block graphs for favourite green fruit, favourite yellow fruit, favourite red fruit, favourite fruit with stones... (**represent data**).

Interpreting the data – sample questions

- Which fruits do you like, not like?
- Which fruits have you eaten, not eaten?
- Which is your favourite fruit on the top row, next row,...?
- Which is your favourite fruit in the left-hand column, the middle column,...?
- In the third row which fruits have stones, have pips?
- Which fruits in the middle column are yellow?
- Which fruits in the middle column do you need to peel?
- How many cherries, plums, peaches,... can you see?
- How many fruits altogether in the first row, third column,...?

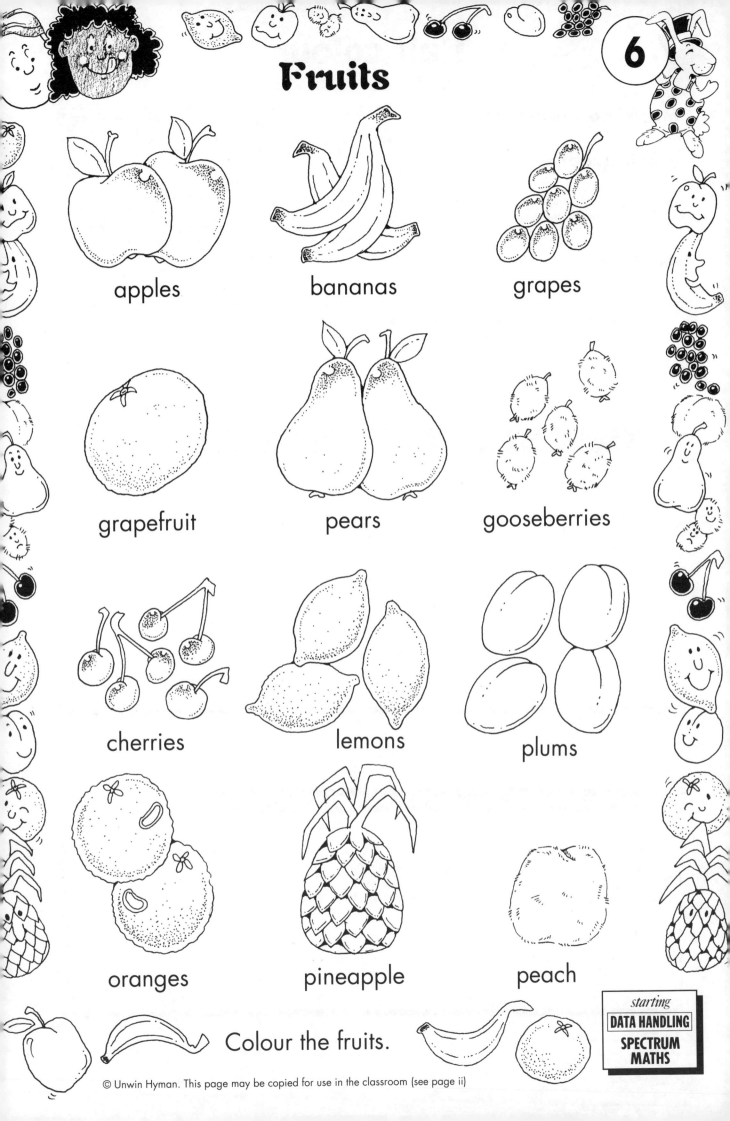

7 Hair colour

Mapping diagrams

Block graphs

Drawing a mapping diagram to show the hair colour of a group of children. Interpreting the diagram.

Activity

Each pupil chooses six children and writes their names in the rectangles. Draw arrows to ovals to indicate hair colour.

LEVEL	Profile Component 1				Profile Component 2		
	UA	N	A	M	UA	S	D
1							●
2							●
3							
4							
5							
6							
7							
8							
9							
10							

D1 Creating and interpreting mapping diagrams.
D2 Block graphs.

Handling the data – sample activities

- Draw another mapping diagram for a different group of six children (**represent data**).

- Draw a block graph to show the distribution of hair colours (**process, represent data**).

- Draw a mapping diagram to show eye colour (**collect, record, represent data**).

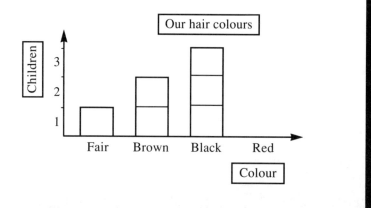

Interpreting the data – sample questions

- Who has fair hair, red hair,...?
- What hair colour has ____ got?
- How many children have black hair, brown hair,...?
- Which hair colour do most of the six children have?
- Which hair colour belongs to two children, three children?

Hair colour

Names   **Colour**

- Fair
- Brown
- Black
- Red

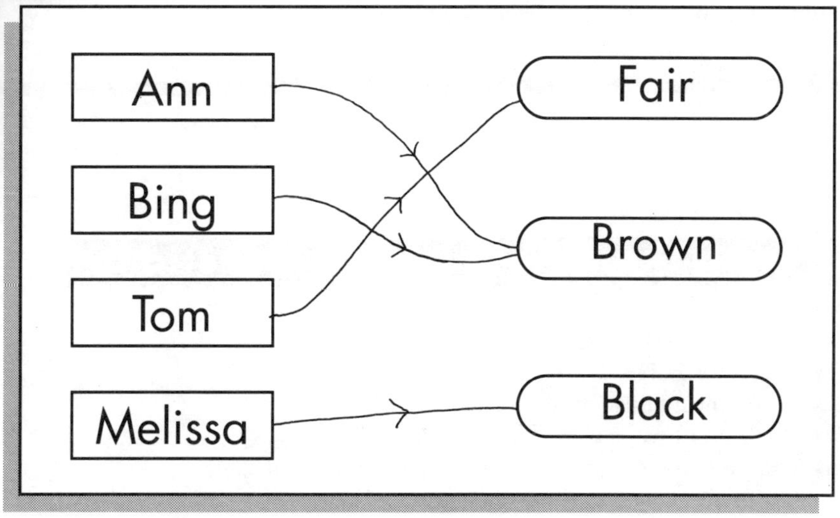

Ann — Fair
Bing — Brown
Tom — (Fair/Brown)
Melissa — Black

Choose five friends. Write your name and their names in the rectangles. Draw lines to show each person's hair colour. Write about the diagram.

starting **DATA HANDLING** **SPECTRUM MATHS**

8 Post

Sorting

Block graphs

Interpreting sorting boxes for the post which are labelled according to groups of letters of the alphabet. Drawing block graphs to show numbers of letters and parcels in each box.

LEVEL	Profile Component 1				Profile Component 2		
	UA	N	A	M	UA	S	D
1					●		●
2					●		●
3					●		
4							
5							
6							
7							
8							
9							
10							

D1 Sorting.
D2 Block graph.

Handling the data – sample activities

- Draw a block graph to show the number of letters in each box (**data representation**).

- Draw a block graph to show the number of parcels in each box (**data representation**).

- Suppose each child in the class is to receive one letter.
  How many in each box? Sort according to:

  a first letter of surname,
  b first letter of first name.

(**Using and applying; collect, process, represent data.**)

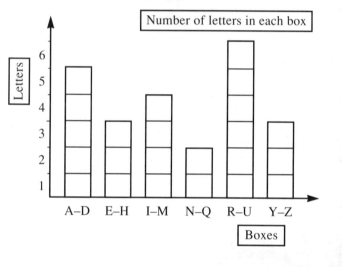

Interpreting the data – sample questions

- How many letters for A–D, I–M,...?
- How many parcels for E–H,...?
- Which box has the most letters, next most letters,...?
- Which box has the most parcels, next most parcels,...?
- How many letters are there altogether on the top shelf, bottom shelf?
- How many parcels are there on the top shelf, bottom shelf?
- How many letters or parcels for W–Z, N–Q,...?
- How many letters of the alphabet for each box?
- Which box has no parcels?
- Which box has eight items, six items,...?

9 Birds

Sorting

Block graphs

Sorting birds' nests according to numbers of eggs, hatched babies, adults for both blackbirds' nests and sparrows' nests. Drawing block graphs to illustrate the different sets of data.

LEVEL	Profile Component 1				Profile Component 2		
	UA	N	A	M	UA	S	D
1							●
2							●
3							
4							
5							
6							
7							
8							
9							
10							

D1 Sorting.
D2 Block graph.

Handling the data – sample activities

- Draw graphs to show:
  a number of eggs/blackbirds' nests
  b number of babies and adults/blackbirds' nests (**represent data**).

- Repeat for sparrows' nests.

- Draw graphs to show the total number of eggs, babies, adults in:
  a blackbirds' nests,
  b sparrows' nests,
  c the whole tree,
  (**process, represent data**).

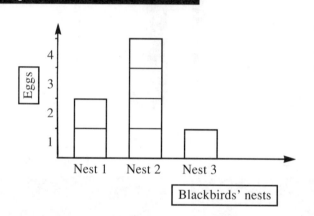

Interpreting the data – sample questions

Four blackbirds
- How many eggs in nest 1, nest 2,...?
- How many babies in nest 1, nest 2,...?
- How many adults in nest 1,...?
- How many blackbird eggs altogether, blackbird adults altogether,...?
- Repeat above type of questions for **sparrows.**
- Which nest has most eggs, no eggs,...?
- How many more sparrows' eggs than blackbirds' eggs?
- Which nest has the most babies, no babies,...?
- When all eggs have been hatched, how many babies in each nest?
- When all eggs are hatched, what is the total number of birds in each nest?

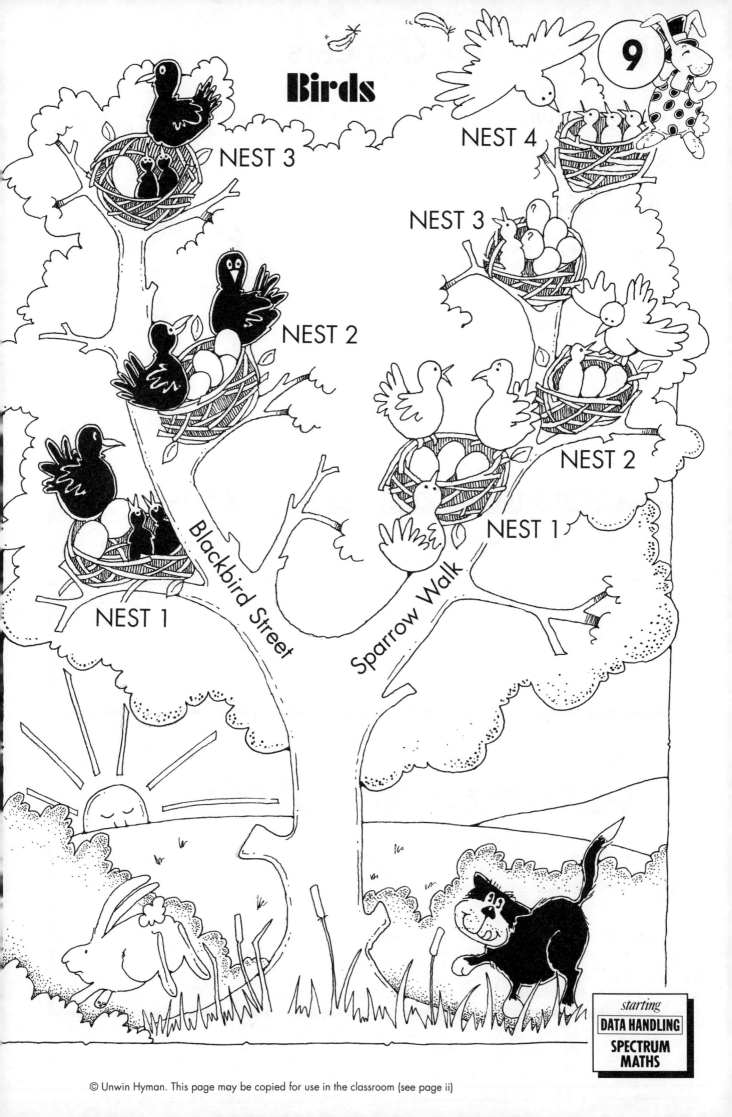

10   Our cars

Picture graphs

Pictograms

Data collection

Interpreting a picture graph showing car colour. Collecting data from a group of pupils and drawing a picture graph.

LEVEL	Profile Component 1				Profile Component 2		
	UA	N	A	M	UA	S	D
1						●	●
2						●	
3						●	●
4							
5							
6							
7							
8							
9							
10							

D1   Picture graph.
D3   Pictogram.

Handling the data – sample activities

- **Collect data** from a group of ten to fifteen pupils on colours of the cars they know best (families' or friends')
  Draw a picture graph to show the results (**represent data**).
  Write some sentences about it (**interpret data**).

- **Collect data** for a larger group of children and draw a pictogram in which one picture represents two cars of that colour. One car can then be represented by 🚗

  (**Using and applying; process, record, represent data**.)

Interpreting the data – sample questions

- How many cars are black, blue,...?
- Which is the colour for exactly two cars, three cars,...?
- How many of the cars are either red or black,...?
- How many cars are there altogether?
- How many cars are not black,...?
- Which colour is the most common, next most common,...?
- How many more cars are black than are white,...?
- What colour is a car you have been in?
- What other car colours are there?

11 Our pets

Picture graphs

Data collection

Interpreting a picture graph showing the pets owned by a group of pupils. Drawing a picture graph for the pupils' own pets.

LEVEL	Profile Component 1				Profile Component 2		
	UA	N	A	M	UA	S	D
1							●
2							
3							
4							
5							
6							
7							
8							
9							
10							

D1 Picture graph.

Handling the data – sample activities

- Pupils **collect data** of pets which they own, then draw a picture graph to show the results (**represent data**). Pupils can be provided with pictures to cut out, sticky shapes, or they can draw the pets themselves.
  Write some sentences about the resulting picture graph (**interpret data**).

- Pupils record the names of their pets alongside the pictures.

Interpreting the data – sample questions

- How many pets are dogs, hamsters,...?
- Which type of pet is owned by exactly four children, three children,...?
- Which pet is the most common, next most common,...?
- How many of the pets are either cats or dogs,...?
- How many pets are there altogether?
- How many of the pets are not dogs,...?
- How many more dogs are there than cats,...?
- How many fewer tortoises than cats,...?
- What other types of pet do children have?

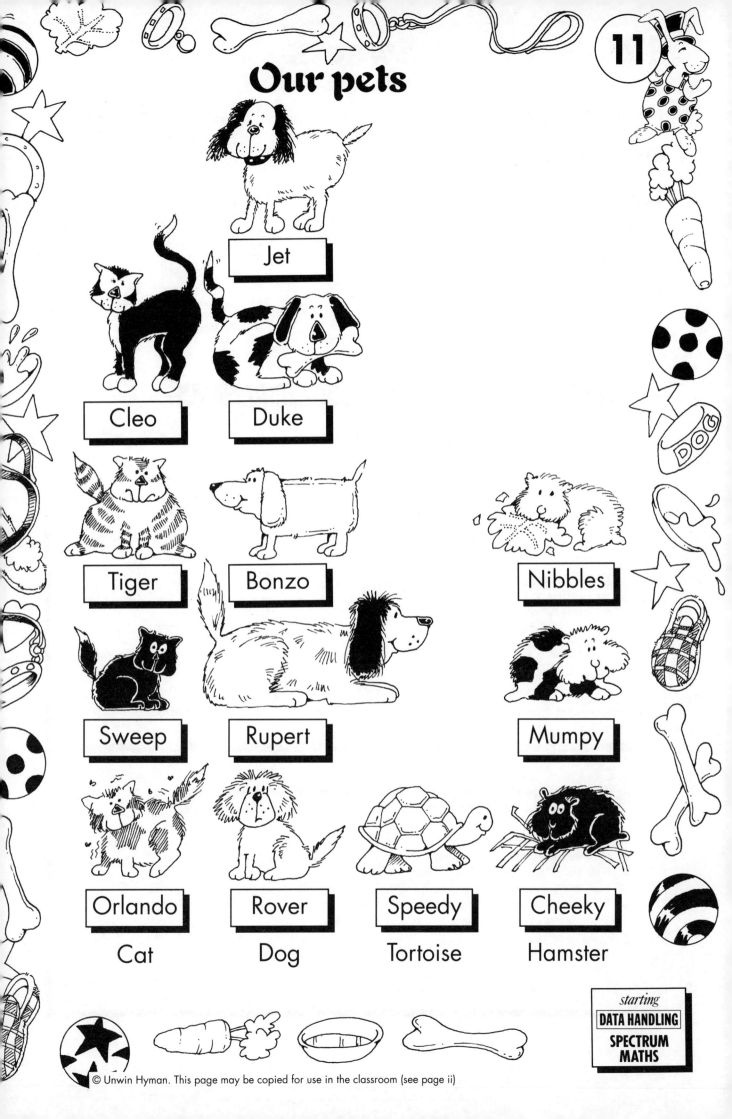

12 Sweets

Picture Graphs

Block Graphs

Tables

Analysing data based on sweets of four different shapes and two sizes. Drawing picture graphs to illustrate the distribution of the different shaped sweets.

LEVEL	Profile Component 1				Profile Component 2		
	UA	N	A	M	UA	S	D
1		●					●
2						●	●
3							●
4							
5							
6							
7							
8							
9							
10							

N1 Counting.
S2 Recognise triangles, squares...
D1 Picture graph.
D2 Block graph.
D3 Tables.

Handling the data – sample activities

- Draw a table to show how many sweets there are of each type (**process data**).

	Large	Small
Square	4	1
Triangle	5	3
Rectangle	2	3
Circle	3	4

- Draw a picture graph to show the different types of large sweets. Repeat for small sweets (**represent data**).

- Draw a block graph to show the distribution of:
  a large sweets,
  b small sweets,
  c large and small sweets together,
  (**represent data**).

- Use a collection of real sweets of different shapes. Analyse the quantities of each shape.

Interpreting the data – sample questions

- What different shapes of sweets can you see?
- How many square-shaped, triangle-shaped,... sweets can you see?
- How many large square-shaped, small square-shaped,... sweets can you see?
- How many more large square-shaped sweets than small square-shaped sweets,... are there ?
- Which large sweets are there the most of: square, rectangular, triangular or circular?
- How many of the large sweets are not triangle-shaped?

Sweets

Write some sentences about this picture.

13 Legs

Recording with objects

Lists

Looking at a picture which contains a number of different objects with differing numbers of legs. Counting the number of legs for each, listing them and recording them using cubes.

LEVEL	Profile Component 1				Profile Component 2		
	UA	N	A	M	UA	S	D
1		●					●
2							
3							●
4							
5							
6							
7							
8							
9							
10							

N1 Counting and ordering.
D1 Recording with objects.
D3 Lists.

Handling the data – sample activities

- Record the number of legs for each object with cubes on a sheet of paper (**record data**).

- Make a list of the different objects in the picture and the number of legs for each (**process, record data**).

- Draw your own picture showing objects with different numbers of legs.

Horse	❏ ❏ ❏ ❏
Child	❏ ❏
Ladybird	❏ ❏ ❏ ❏ ❏ ❏

Interpreting the data – sample questions

- Where is the ladybird? How many legs does it have?
- Can you see something with three legs?
- How many objects can you see with four legs?
- Which objects have more than four legs?
- Which objects have less than three legs?
- Which objects have an odd number of legs?
- Which object has the most/least number of legs?
- How many more legs does the ladybird have than the horse?
- How many less legs does the horse have than the caterpillar?

14 Fish tank

Frequency tables

Counting the number of different types of creature in a fish tank. Recording the numbers in a table.

LEVEL	Profile Component 1				Profile Component 2		
	UA	N	A	M	UA	S	D
1		●			●		
2					●		●
3					●		
4							
5							
6							
7							
8							
9							
10							

N1 Counting and ordering.
D2 Frequency tables.

Handling the data – sample activities

- Construct a frequency table to show the number of each object in the tank (**process, record data**). Write something about the table (**interpret data**).

- Draw your own fish tank and its contents. Construct a table to show the number of each object (**using and applying; process, record data**).

Octopuses	✗ ✗
Crab	✗ ✗ ✗
Fish	✗ ✗ ✗ ✗
Shells	✗ ✗ ✗ ✗ ✗
Sea-horses	✗ ✗ ✗

Interpreting the data – sample questions

- How many crabs, octopuses,... can you see?
- How many more fish then crabs?
- How many fewer octopuses than shells?
- Are there more or fewer sea-horses than shells? How many more? How many fewer?
- How many of the fish are swimming to the left, how many to the right?

Fish tank

Write some sentences about the picture.

15 Drinks

Tables

Data collection

Interpreting a table showing likes and dislikes of five children based on five drinks. Collection and analysis of similar data from pupils in the class.

LEVEL	Profile Component 1				Profile Component 2		
	UA	N	A	M	UA	S	D
1					●		
2					●		
3					●		●
4							
5							
6							
7							
8							
9							
10							

D3 Tables.

Handling the data – sample activities

- **Collect data** from a group of five children on their likes and dislikes about these five drinks. Construct a table to show the results (**process data**).

- Consider a different set of drinks, list them, collect data of likes and dislikes, and represent it in a table (**collect, process, record, represent data**).

- Design a table for foods instead of drinks, then collect some data and analyse it (**using and applying; collect, process, record, represent, interpret data**).

Interpreting the data – sample questions

- Which drinks does Hamish like, not like?
- How many of the drinks does Mina like, not like?
- Who likes all five drinks?
- Which drink does everyone like?
- How many children like milk, orange juice,...?
- Which children like tea, water,...?
- How many children don't like water, tea,...?
- Which drink is the most popular, least popular,...?
- Who likes the least number of drinks?
- Which of these drinks do you like?

Drinks

Drinks we like

	Milk	Lemonade	Water	Tea	Orange juice
Hamish	✗	✓	✓	✗	✗
Mina	✓	✓	✓	✓	✓
Katie	✗	✓	✗	✗	✓
Amil	✓	✓	✓	✗	✓
Emily	✗	✓	✓	✗	✓

Write some sentences about this table.

16 Odds or evens

Recording with objects

Block graphs

Chance

LEVEL	Profile Component 1				Profile Component 2		
	UA	N	A	M	UA	S	D
1					●		●
2			●		●		●
3					●		●
4							
5							
6							
7							
8							
9							
10							

Throwing a single dice several times and recording the outcome in terms of 'odd number' or 'even number'.

A2 Odds and evens.
D1 Recording with real objects.
D2 Block graphs.
D3 Two equally likely events of chance.

Apparatus

Use a dice numbered 1–6 and a set of counters.

Activity

Pupils throw the dice, then place a counter on the sheet, according to whether the number is odd or even. Continue until a line of counters reaches the top.

Handling the data – sample activities

- In pairs, one pupil can choose 'odd', another 'even'.
  Repeat the activity several times to see who wins the most often (**collect data**).

- **Represent data** by drawing block graphs to show the outcome of each throw. Use sticky circles for blocks.

- Repeat the activity with a dice numbered differently e.g. number the faces of a cube, 1, 3, 4, 5, 6, 7 (**using and applying**).

Interpreting the data – sample questions

- Which dice numbers are odd, which are even?
- How many times did the dice show an odd number?
- How many times did the dice show an even number?
- Which occurred most, odd or even? By how much?
- How many throws did you have altogether?
- What do you think will happen if you repeat the activity?

Odds or evens

Use a dice numbered 1–6, and a set of counters.

Odd number	Even number

Throw the dice. Look at the number and place a counter in the correct column, starting from the bottom upwards. Continue until one of the columns is full.

starting **DATA HANDLING** SPECTRUM MATHS

17 Linking dots

Mapping diagrams

Drawing mapping diagrams to link sets of dots according to:
a   has the same number of dots and
b   has dots which sum to ten.

LEVEL	Profile Component 1				Profile Component 2		
	UA	N	A	M	UA	S	D
1		●					●
2					●		
3					●		
4							
5							
6							
7							
8							
9							
10							

N1   Counting.
D1   Create and interpret mapping diagrams.

Handling the data – sample activities

- **Represent data** by drawing mapping lines to join the sets on the left with the sets on the right according to 'has the same number of dots as'.

- **Represent data** by drawing mapping lines according to 'has dots which sum to ten'.

- Invent your own sets of dots and draw mapping lines (**using and applying**).

Interpreting the data – sample questions

- How many dots in the first, second,... set on the left?
- How many dots in the first, second,... set on the right?
- Which sets have four dots, six dots,...?
- Which sets have an odd number of dots, even number of dots?
- How many dots need to be added to this set to make ten?
- Which sets have more than seven dots, fewer than four dots,...?
- Which sets have between six and nine dots?
- How many dots need to be added to this set to make eight?

18 Twenty coins

Sorting

Block graphs

Sorting a set of coins into different types: 1p, 2p, 5p, 10p and 20p. Drawing a block graph to show the number of each type.

LEVEL	Profile Component 1				Profile Component 2		
	UA	N	A	M	UA	S	D
1							●
2		●					●
3							
4							
5							
6							
7							
8							
9							
10							

N2 Solving money problems.
D1 Sorting.
D2 Block graphs.

Handling the data – sample activities

- **Represent data** by drawing a graph to show the number of times each coin appears.

- Make a collection of coins, spread them out on the table, then draw a graph to show the quantity of each type (**collect, process, represent data**).

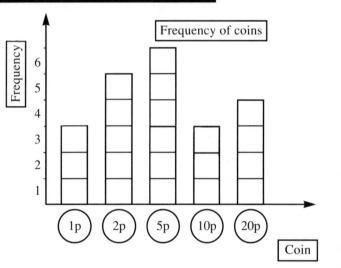

Interpreting the data – sample questions

- How many 10p coins, 5p coins,... can you see?
- How many different types of coins are there?
- For which coin is there most, next most,...?
- What is the total value of all the 1p coins,...?
- How many more 1p coins than 2p coins,... are there?

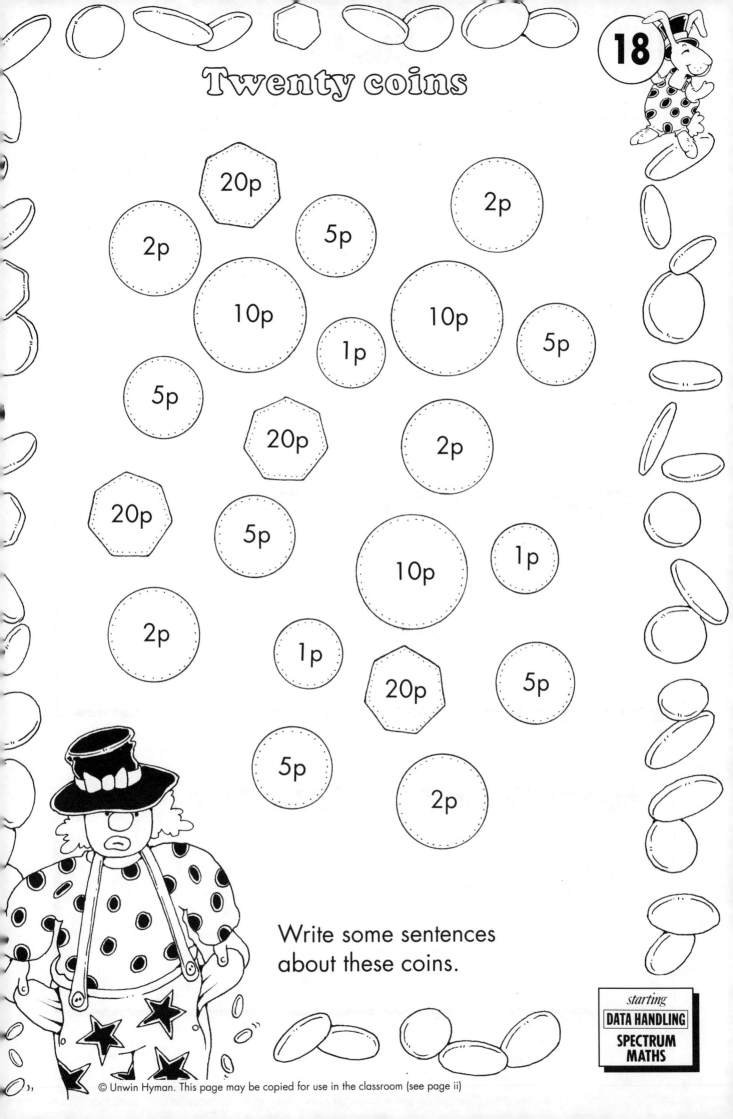

19 Clocks

Sorting

Reading clock faces' showing times on the hour. Ordering the times. Sorting the clock faces into sets.

LEVEL	Profile Component 1				Profile Component 2		
	UA	N	A	M	UA	S	D
1							●
2							
3				●			
4							
5							
6							
7							
8							
9							
10							

M3 Reading clocks.
D1 Sorting and ordering.

Handling the data – sample activities

- Cut out the clocks and arrange them in order of time (**process data**).

- Sort the clocks into sets,
  e.g. before 6 o'clock, not before 6 o'clock,
  between 3 o'clock and 9 o'clock, not between 3 o'clock and 9 o'clock,
  square faces, triangular faces, circular faces, hexagonal faces.

Interpreting the data – sample questions

- What is the time on clock A, E,...?
- Which clock shows 4 o'clock, 7 o'clock,...?
- Which clocks show a time before 6 o'clock?
- Which clocks show a time after 9 o'clock?
- How many clocks show a time after 7 o'clock?
- Which clock shows the latest time on the top row, second row,...?
- Which clock shows the earliest time on the left-hand column, the middle column,...?
- Which clocks show a time when you are in school? Which when you are at home?

Clocks

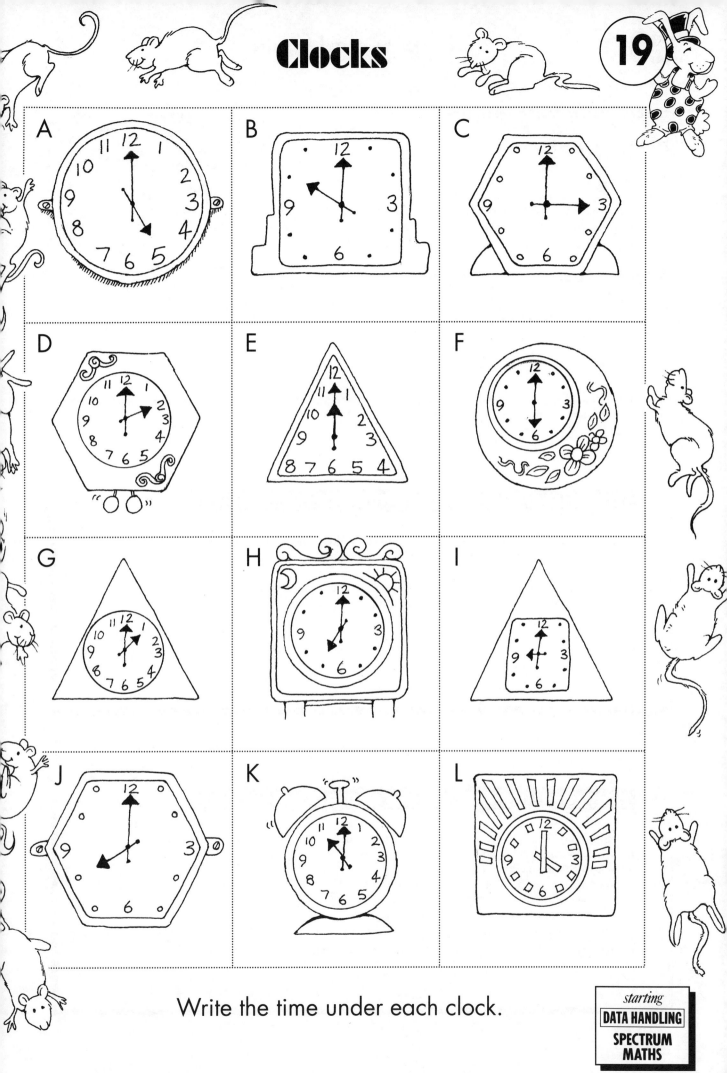

Write the time under each clock.

20 Three colours

Recording with objects
Block graphs
Chance

Throwing a single dice whose faces are coloured red, blue and yellow; two of each. Recording the outcomes using counters.

LEVEL	Profile Component 1				Profile Component 2		
	UA	N	A	M	UA	S	D
1					●		●
2					●		●
3					●		●
4							
5							
6							
7							
8							
9							
10							

D1 Recording with real objects.
D2 Block graphs.
D3 Three equally likely events of chance.

Apparatus

Use a cube with coloured faces: two red, two blue, and two yellow. You also need some red, blue and yellow counters.

Activity

Pupils throw the dice, and according to the colour shown place a counter in the appropriate column, starting from the bottom upwards. Continue until one of the lines is complete.

Handling the data - sample activities

- In threes, each pupil chooses one of red, blue or yellow. The activity thus becomes a competition to see who wins. Repeat the activity several times (**collect data**).

- **Represent data** by drawing block graphs to illustrate the results. Use sticky squares or circles for blocks. Write about the graph (**interpret data**).

Interpreting the data - sample questions

- How many times did the dice show red, blue, yellow?
- Which colour appeared most often, next most often,...?
- Which colour appeared four times,...?
- How many more times did yellow show than red,...?
- How many fewer times did blue show than yellow,...?
- How many of the throws showed red or blue, yellow or blue,...?
- How many throws were there altogether?
- What do you think will happen if you repeated the activity?

Three colours

20

Use a cube with coloured faces: two red, two blue, two yellow. You also need some red, blue and yellow counters.

Red   Blue   Yellow

Throw the dice. Look at the colour and place the counter in the correct column, starting from the bottom upwards. Continue until one of the columns is full.

starting **DATA HANDLING** SPECTRUM MATHS

21 Jungle

Recording with objects

Lists

Counting the number of different animals in a picture of the jungle. Listing the animals and recording the number of each with counters.

LEVEL	Profile Component 1				Profile Component 2		
	UA	N	A	M	UA	S	D
1		●			●		●
2					●		
3					●		●
4							
5							
6							
7							
8							
9							
10							

N1 Counting.
D1 Recording with objects.
D3 Lists.

Handling the data – sample activities

- Make a list of the different animals and record the number of each type with counters (**record, process data**).

- Draw your own picture containing different numbers of animals. Then make a list to show the number of each (**using and applying**).

Monkeys ○ ○ ○ ○ ○

Bears ○ ○ ○

Parrots ○ ○

Interpreting the data – sample questions

- How many bears, snakes,... can you see?
- Which animals are there three of?
- Which animals are there more than three of?
- Of which animal are there most, fewest?
- How many more monkeys than snakes can you see?
- How many fewer snakes than bears?
- How many bears and tigers altogether?
- How many animals altogether?

22 Cards

Tables

Blocks graphs

Analysing a set of ten playing cards in terms of their suit, and their number. Drawing block graphs to illustrate the results.

LEVEL	Profile Component 1				Profile Component 2		
	UA	N	A	M	UA	S	D
1					●		
2					●		●
3					●		●
4							
5							
6							
7							
8							
9							
10							

D2 Block graphs.
D3 Tables.

Handling the data – sample activities

- Complete the block graph showing the number of cards in each suit (**record data**). Write some sentences about it (**interpret data**).

- Draw a table showing the number in each suit (**process, represent data**).

- Shuffle a pack of playing cards, deal out ten from the top of the pile and draw a block graph to show the number in each suit (**using and applying; collect, record, represent data**).

	H	C	D	S
2	✔		✔	✔
3		✔		
4	✔			
5	✔		✔	
6		✔	✔	

Interpreting the data – sample questions

- Where is the two of hearts, five of diamonds,...?
- How many hearts, clubs,... can you see?
- Which are the spades?
- Which suit has the most, fewest cards on the sheet?
- How many cards are there altogether?
- How many more diamonds cards than hearts cards can you see?
- How many clubs and spades cards are there altogether?
- How many of the cards are not diamonds?

Cards

Colour the blocks to show the number of cards in each suit. Write some sentences about it.

23 Shape sort

Sorting

Block graphs

Sorting a set of shapes into different types: circles, squares, rectangles, triangles. Drawing a block graph to illustrate the data.

LEVEL	Profile Component 1				Profile Component 2		
	UA	N	A	M	UA	S	D
1					●		●
2					●	●	●
3					●		
4							
5							
6							
7							
8							
9							
10							

S2 Recognition of plane shapes.
D1 Sorting.
D2 Block graphs.

Handling the data – sample activities

- Complete the block graph showing the quantity of each shape. These blocks can be shaded in the same colours as the shapes (**represent data**).

- Take a random collection of logiblocks and draw a block graph to show the distribution of the different shapes (**using and applying; collect record, represent data**).

Interpreting the data – sample questions

- How many different shapes can you see?
- What are the names of the different shapes?
- How many squares, triangles,... are there?
- For which shape is there most, fewest?
- How many more circles than squares are there?
- How many fewer rectangles than triangles are there?

Shape sort

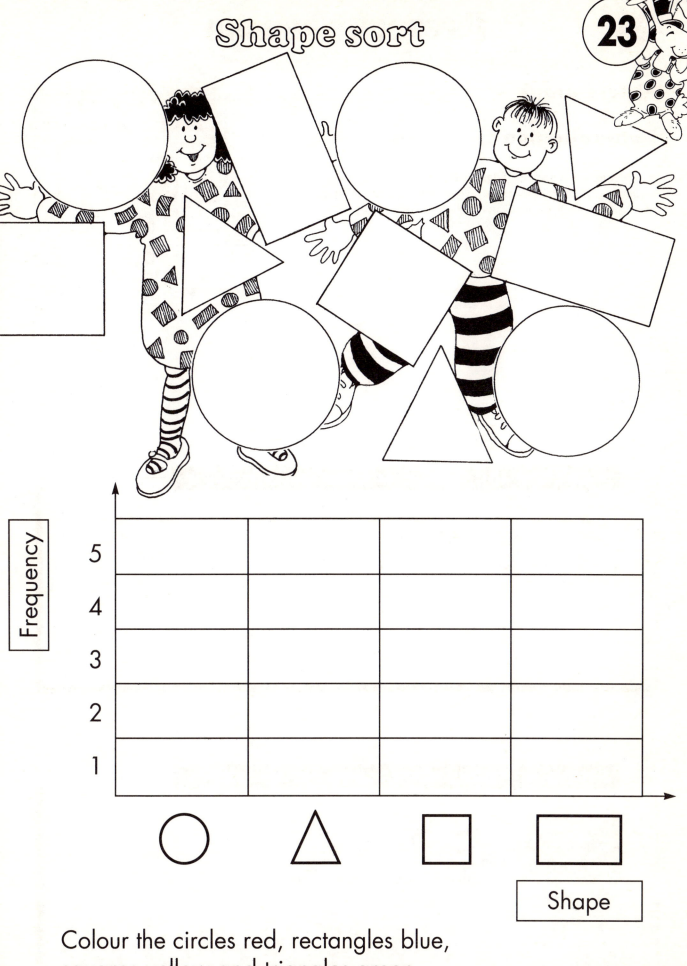

Colour the circles red, rectangles blue, squares yellow and triangles green.

24 Favourite season

Picture graph

Data collection

Interpreting a picture graph relating to a group of children's favourite season. Collection of data and creating a picture graph from choices made by pupils in the class.

LEVEL	Profile Component 1				Profile Component 2		
	UA	N	A	M	UA	S	D
1		●					●
2							
3							
4							
5							
6							
7							
8							
9							
10							

N1 Counting.
D1 Picture graph.

Handling the data – sample activities

- **Collect data** from a group of children about their favourite season. Make a picture graph to show the preferences (**represent data**). Write some sentences about the graph (**interpret data**).

- Pupils write about why they prefer a particular season.

Interpreting the data – sample questions

- How many children prefer spring, summer,...?
- Which children prefer winter, summer,...?
- Which season do Aziz, Mandy, Wesley,... prefer?
- How many children altogether?
- How many children like spring or summer, summer or autumn,...?
- How many children do not prefer spring,...?

25 Ice cream

Picture graph

Block graph

Pictogram

Data collection

Interpreting a picture graph and block graph which illustrate a group of children's favourite flavour of ice cream. Collecting data for favourite flavour from the class and drawing the corresponding picture graph and block graph.

LEVEL	Profile Component 1				Profile Component 2		
	UA	N	A	M	UA	S	D
1		●			●		●
2					●		●
3					●		●
4							
5							
6							
7							
8							
9							
10							

N1 Ordering numbers; counting.
D1 Picture graph.
D2 Block graph.
D3 Pictogram.

Handling the data – sample activities

- Groups of children **collect data** on their favourite flavour, then draw both a picture graph and a block graph to illustrate the results (**represent data**). Write some sentences about it (**interpret data**).

- **Collect data** for the whole class and draw a pictogram in which represents two votes and represents one vote (**represent data**).

Interpreting the data – sample questions

- How many children prefer strawberry, mint,...?
- Which is the most popular, next most popular,... flavour?
- How many fewer prefer mint to vanilla,...?
- How many more prefer chocolate to mint,...?
- How many children voted altogether?
- How many did not prefer vanilla,...?
- How many preferred either strawberry or chocolate,...?
- What other ice cream flavours are there?

26 Crisps

Picture graph

Block graph

Data collection

Interpreting a picture graph showing a group of children's choices of flavour of crisps. Collecting data of choices of flavour from groups within the class and constructing a picture graph.

LEVEL	Profile Component 1				Profile Component 2		
	UA	N	A	M	UA	S	D
1						●	●
2						●	●
3						●	
4							
5							
6							
7							
8							
9							
10							

D1 Picture graph.
D2 Block graph.

Handling the data – sample activities

- **Collect data** by asking pupils to choose their favourite flavour of crisps. Draw a picture graph to illustrate the results and then write some sentences about the graph (**represent, interpret data**). Draw a block graph to illustrate the data.

- Try similar activities for favourite chocolate bars.

- Place four different types of crisp on each of four plates. Blindfold the children who then taste each flavour and choose their favourite. Analyse the results (**using and applying**).

Interpreting the data – sample questions

- Who chose salt 'n vinegar, plain,...?
- What flavour did John, Yasmin,... choose?
- How many children chose salt 'n vinegar, smokey bacon,...?
- Which flavour was the most popular, next most popular,...?
- How many children altogether?
- How many chose either plain or smokey bacon,...?
- How many children did not choose plain,...?
- What other flavours of crisps are there?

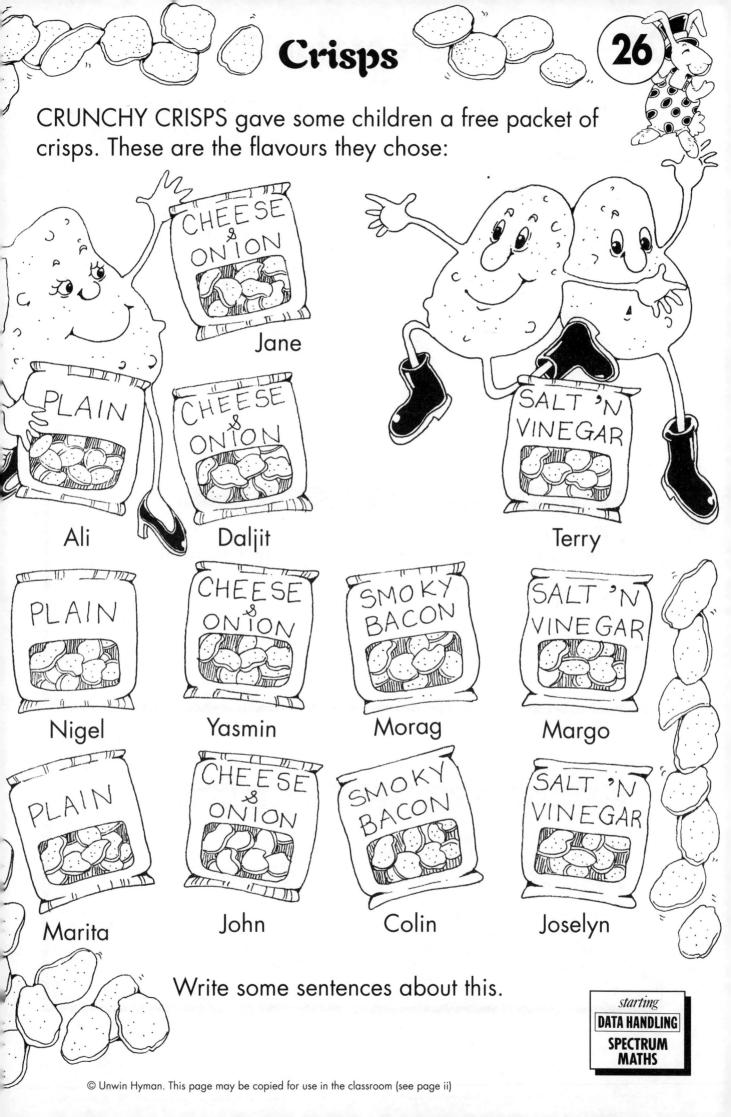

27 Left or right?

Carroll diagram

Data collection

Interpreting a Carroll diagram for boys/girls v left/right-handedness. Collecting data and drawing a Carroll diagram for a group of pupils using the same criteria for classification.

LEVEL	Profile Component 1				Profile Component 2		
	UA	N	A	M	UA	S	D
1					●		
2					●		●
3					●		
4							
5							
6							
7							
8							
9							
10							

D2   Carroll diagrams.

Handling the data – sample activities

- **Collect data** for a group of children and draw a Carroll diagram, writing the names in the appropriate cells. Write some sentences about the diagram (**represent, interpret data**).

- Draw Carroll diagrams based on different criteria.
  Examples include:

  Hair: curly/straight v long/short,
  Beetroot: boys/girls v likes/dislikes beetroot,
  (**collect, record, interpret data**).

Interpreting the data – sample questions

- How many left-handed boys, right-handed girls,...?
- Is Jenny, Jacob,... left-handed or right-handed?
- Who is a left-handed girl, left-handed boy,...?
- Which girls are not right-handed?
- How many girls altogether, boys altogether?
- How many children altogether?
- How many left-handed altogether, right-handed altogether?
- Which group has two children, three children,...?
- How many more right-handed than left-handed children are there?

Left or right?

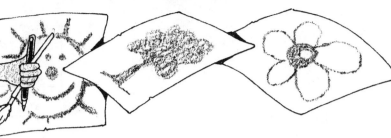

	Boys	Girls
Left-handed	Stanley	Karen Shireen
Right-handed	Jacob Gurdeep Peter	Jenny Fatima Honor Tracey

starting DATA HANDLING SPECTRUM MATHS

28 Tables

Tables

Lists

Studying a multiplication table showing multiplication facts up to 5 × 5.
Ordering the products.

LEVEL	Profile Component 1				Profile Component 2		
	UA	N	A	M	UA	S	D
1							
2							
3		●	●				●
4		●					
5							
6							
7							
8							
9							
10							

N3/N4   Multiplication facts.
A3   Number patterns.
D3   Tables. Lists.

Handling the data - sample activities

- Make a list of the different numbers in the table. Put them in order:

    1, 2, 3, 4, 5, 6, 8, 9, 10, 12, 15, 16, 20,

    (**record, process data**).

- Draw a new table, but extend it to include multiplying by 6. Analyse the numbers in the table.

×	1	2	3	4	5	6
1	1	2	3	4	5	6
2	2	4	6	8	10	12
3	3	6	9	12	15	18
4	4	8	12	16	20	24
5	5	10	15	20	25	30
6	6	12	18	24	30	36

Interpreting the data - sample questions

- What numbers are in the 1st row, 2nd row,...?
- What numbers are in the 1st column, 2nd column,...?
- What is 3 × 2, 4 × 3,...?
- Can you say the numbers in the 3rd row without looking?
- What is the largest number in the table?
- Which numbers occur twice?
- Which numbers occur only once?
- What patterns can you see along the rows, down the columns?
- What patterns can you see along the diagonals?

Tables

X	1	2	3	4	5
1	1	2	3	4	5
2	2	4	6	8	10
3	3	6	9	12	15
4	4	8	12	16	20
5	5	10	15	20	25

29 Pencils

Sorting

Lists

Comparison of the lengths of eight pencils. Measuring their lengths in centimetres and ordering them from largest to shortest.

LEVEL	Profile Component 1				Profile Component 2		
	UA	N	A	M	UA	S	D
1							●
2							
3				●			●
4							
5							
6							
7							
8							
9							
10							

M3 Using centimetres.
D1 Sorting.
D3 Lists.

Handling the data – sample activities

- Write 'first', 'second', 'third' alongside each pencil to indicate the longest, next longest,... and so on (**process data**).

- Make a list showing the length of each pencil (**record data**).

Pencil	Length
Red	10 cm
Blue	6 cm
Black	8 cm

Interpreting the data – sample questions

- How many pencils are there altogether?
- Which pencil is the longest, next longest?
- Which pencil is the shortest, next shortest?
- How long is the blue, green,... pencil?
- Which pencil is 6 cm long, 3 cm long,...?
- Which pencils are more than 6 cm long?
- Which pencils are less than 5 cm long?
- How much longer is the black pencil than the yellow pencil?
- How much shorter is the white pencil than the purple pencil?

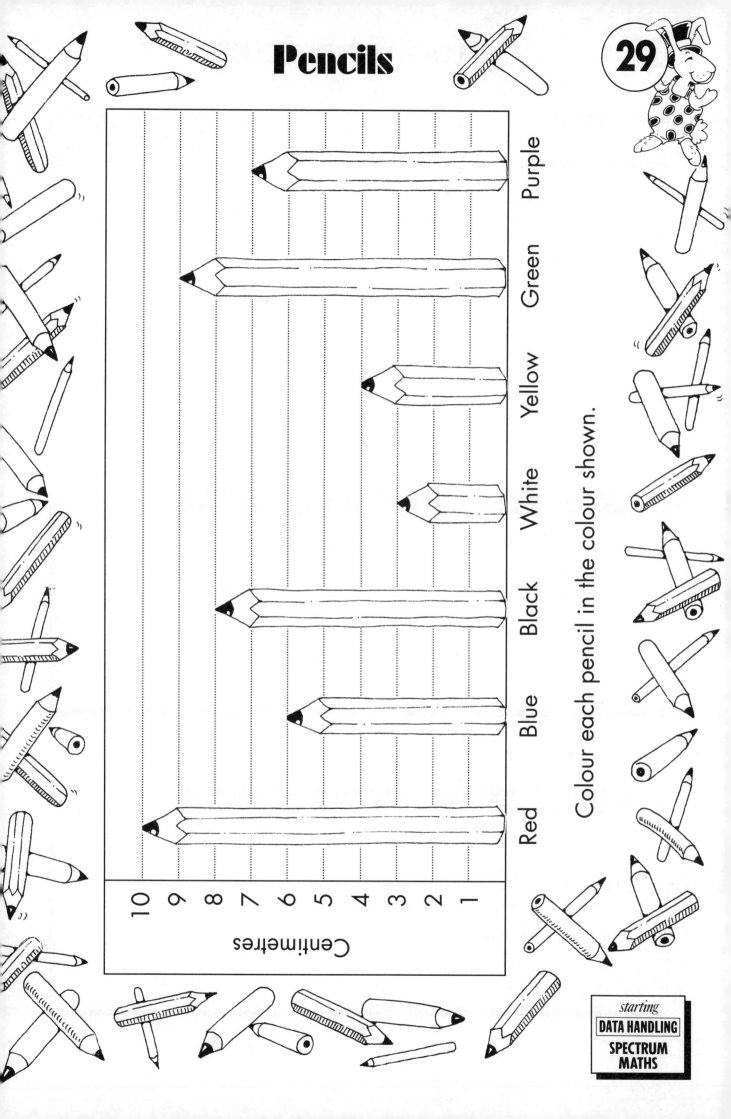

30 Cartoon characters

Block graphs

Data collection

Interpreting a block graph showing favourite cartoon characters. Collecting data from the pupils and illustrating the results with a block graph.

LEVEL	Profile Component 1				Profile Component 2		
	UA	N	A	M	UA	S	D
1		●			●		
2					●		●
3					●		
4							
5							
6							
7							
8							
9							
10							

N1 Ordering. Counting.
D2 Block graphs.

Handling the data - sample activities

- Make a list of different cartoon characters (**collect data**).

- **Collect, record data** on pupils' favourite TV cartoon character. Draw a graph to illustrate the results (**represent data**). Write some sentences about the graph (**interpret data**).

Interpreting the data - sample questions

- How many different cartoon characters are listed?
- How many children voted for Mouse, Duck,...?
- Which character had three votes, six votes,...?
- Who is the most popular, next most popular,...?
- Who had more than four votes, less than five votes,...?
- Who is your favourite?
- Which other cartoon characters do you know?

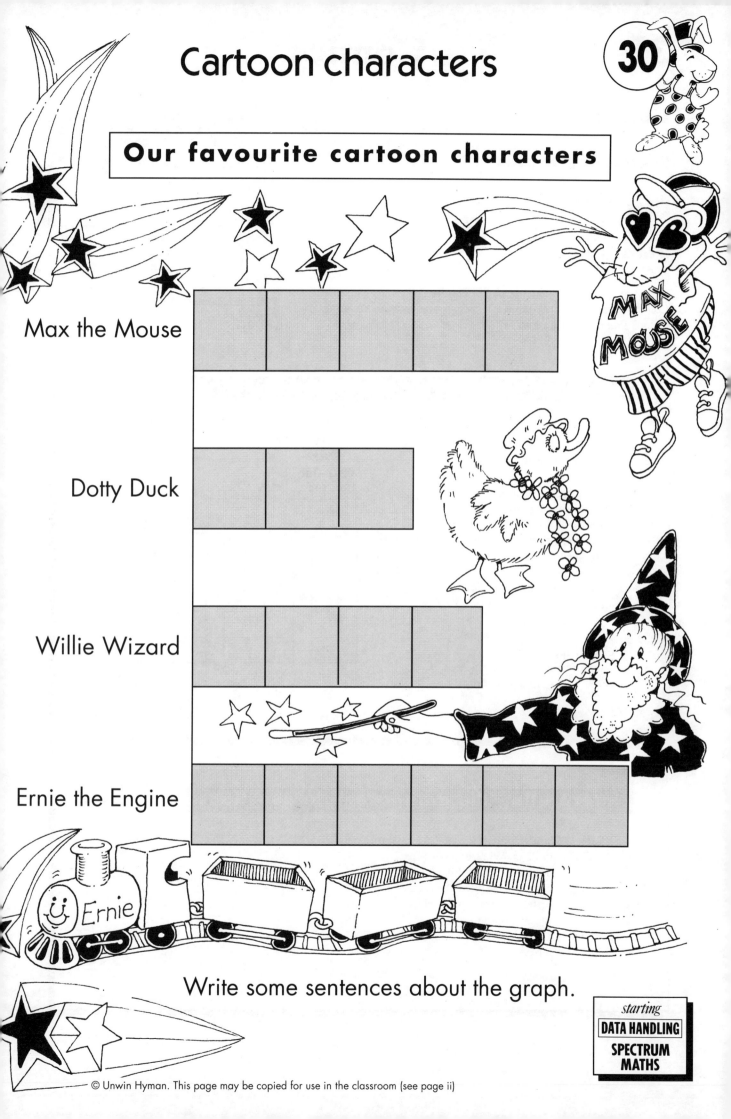

31 Comics

Block graphs

Frequency tables

Lists

Data collection

Interpreting a list showing a group of children's favourite comics. Constructing a frequency table to condense the data and drawing a block graph to illustrate it.

LEVEL	Profile Component 1				Profile Component 2		
	UA	N	A	M	UA	S	D
1					●		
2					●		●
3					●		●
4							
5							
6							
7							
8							
9							
10							

D2 Block Graphs. Frequency tables.
D3 Lists.

Handling the data – sample activities

- Draw a table to record the number of votes for each comic (**process, record data**).

- Draw a block graph to illustrate the number of votes for each (**represent data**).
  Write some sentences about it (**interpret data**).

- **Collect data** from pupils in the class regarding their favourite comics and analyse the data. Bring some comics to school. Collect and analyse data on favourite characters within each comic (**using and applying**).

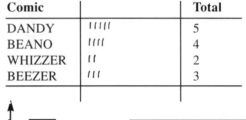

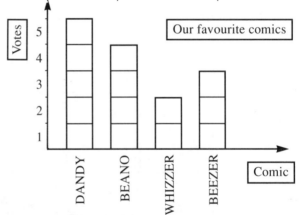

Interpreting the data – sample questions

- Which is Clare's, Farouk's, Lynn's,... favourite comic?
- Whose favourite is 'Whizzer and Chips'?
- How many children like the Beano best?
- How many children are there altogether?
- How many different comics were chosen?
- How many more children voted for Dandy than Beano,...?
- How many children did not vote for Dandy?
- Which is your favourite?

Our favourite comics

Aaron	DANDY
Bernadette	WHIZZER AND CHIPS
Clare	BEANO
Daljit	BEANO
Erica	BEEZER
Farouk	DANDY
Gary	WHIZZER AND CHIPS
Harriet	DANDY
Ivan	BEEZER
Jasminder	BEEZER
Kate	DANDY
Lynn	BEANO
Maya	DANDY
Nazdeep	BEANO

starting
DATA HANDLING
SPECTRUM MATHS

32 Car numbers

Frequency tables
Bar graphs
Data collection

Constructing a frequency table based on the occurrence of digits in a set of car registration numbers. Interpreting the results and drawing a bar graph to represent them.

Activity

Draw a frequency table to find the number of times each digit occurs in the number plates. Draw a bar graph to illustrate the results.

Digit		Total
0	⊬⊬⊬ l	6
1		
2		

Digit	0	1	2	3	4	5	6	7	8	9
Freq	3	1	3	4	6	3	7	9	4	5

LEVEL	Profile Component 1				Profile Component 2		
	UA	N	A	M	UA	S	D
1					●		
2					●		●
3					●		●
4							
5							
6							
7							
8							
9							
10							

D2 Frequency tables.
D3 Bar graphs.

Handling the data – sample activities

- Draw a bar graph to show the frequency of digit occurrence in the car numbers (**represent data**).

- Collect another set of car numbers from the school car park, or cars passing in the road. construct a frequency table and comment on the results (**using and applying; collect, record, process, interpret data**).

- Analyse the letter frequency in the registration numbers.

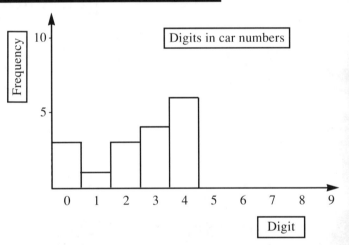

Digits in car numbers

Interpreting the data – sample questions

- How many 1s, 3s,...?
- Which digit occurs ____ times, ____ times?
- Which digit occurs most frequently, next most frequently,...?
- Which is the most frequent odd digit, even digit?
- How many more 7s than 2s?
- How many less 3s than 9s?

Car numbers

32

E 379 GXT

C 645 KHE

F 491 TRT

NRX 909 X

E 257 VWJ

AOX 466 T

RVP 404 Y

EWF 676 V

PKU 876 X

D 397 JYL

UWJ 872 V

C 785 LWJ

F 463 SYD

E 832 PKY

D 670 OWG

Which numbers appear most often on the registration plates?

starting
DATA HANDLING
SPECTRUM MATHS

© Unwin Hyman. This page may be copied for use in the classroom (see page ii)

33 Activities

Tables

Block graphs

Data collection

Interpreting a two-way table showing four children's likes and dislikes in three activities. Collecting class data and constructing similar tables. Drawing block graphs to illustrate the results.

LEVEL	Profile Component 1				Profile Component 2		
	UA	N	A	M	UA	S	D
1					●		
2					●		●
3					●		●
4							
5							
6							
7							
8							
9							
10							

D2 Block graphs.
D3 Tables.

Handling the data – sample activities

- **Process data** by writing down the totals for each row and column.

- Draw a block graph to show how many children like football, swimming, dancing (**represent data**).
  Write some sentences about it (**interpret data**).

- Draw a graph to show how many activities each child likes (**represent data**).

- **Collect data** for a group of pupils and represent it in table form (**process data**). Then analyse it.

	Likes football	Likes swimming	Likes dancing	Total
Guy	✓	✓	✓	3
Charanjit	✗	✗	✓	1
Penny	✓	✗	✓	2
Alaistair	✓	✗	✗	1
Total	3	1	3	7

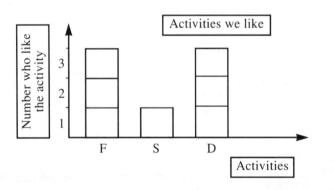

Interpreting the data – sample questions

- What does Charanjit, Guy,... like, not like?
- Who likes football, dancing,...?
- How many activities does Penny, Alaistair,... like?
- How many children like swimming, dancing,...?
- How many children don't like football, swimming,...?
- Who likes the most activities? Who the fewest?
- What is the most popular activity, next most popular,...?
- How many more children like dancing than like football?
- Which activities do you like?

Activities

	Likes football	Likes swimming	Likes dancing
Guy	✔	✔	✔
Charanjit	✘	✘	✔
Penny	✔	✘	✔
Alaistair	✔	✘	✘

Write down the number of ticks for each row and each column. Write some sentences about it.

starting **DATA HANDLING** SPECTRUM MATHS

© Unwin Hyman. This page may be copied for use in the classroom (see page ii)

34 Ladybirds

Sorting

Tables

Counting the number of spots on a set of ladybirds. Sorting them into sets in table form.

LEVEL	Profile Component 1					Profile Component 2		
	UA	N	A	M	UA	S	D
1		●					●
2			●				
3							●
4							
5							
6							
7							
8							
9							
10							

N1 Counting.
A2 Even numbers.
D1 Sorting.
D3 Tables.

Handling the data – sample activities

- Make a table showing the number of spots for each ladybird (**process data**).
- Pupils draw their own set of ladybirds and name them.

2 spots	4 spots	6 spots	8 spots	10 spots
Lucy	Lulu Lorraine Lynn Lorna	Lotte Lesley	Lena	Lilly

Interpreting the data – sample questions

- How many spots does Lynn, Lena,... have?
- Who has six spots, two spots,...?
- Who has the most spots?
- Who has the fewest spots?
- Who has an odd number, even number of spots?
- How many spots does Lucy,... have on each side?
- Which ladybird has the longest name?
- Which row of ladybirds has the most spots altogether?

Ladybirds

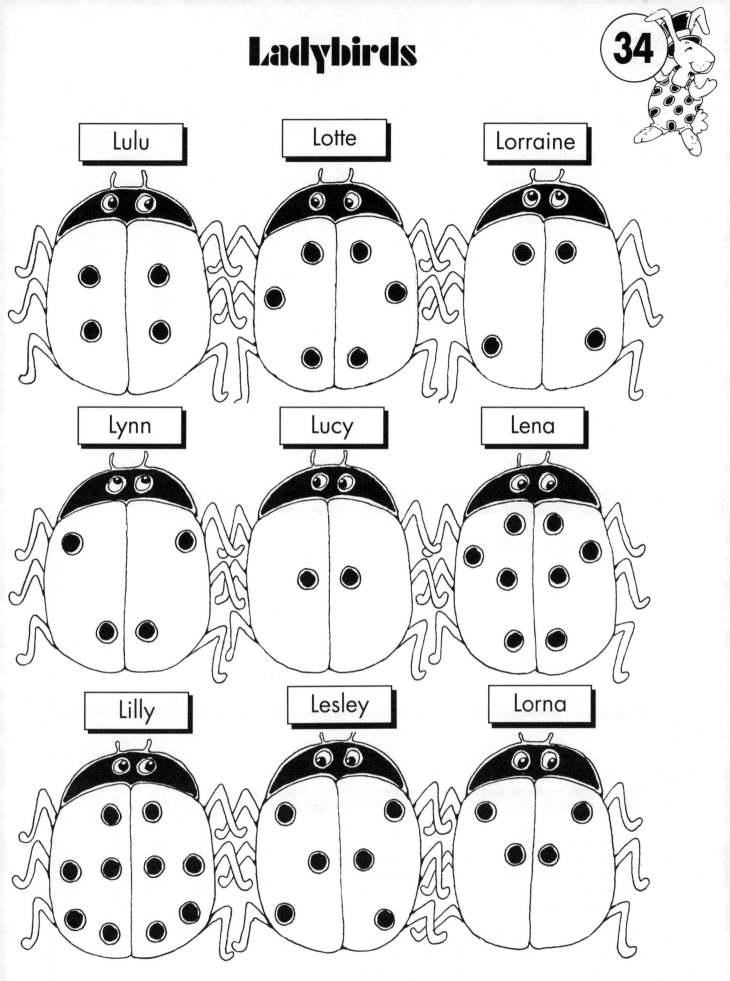

How many spots on each ladybird?

35 Coin maps

Mapping diagrams

Drawing mapping diagrams joining sets of coins to sums of money.

LEVEL	Profile Component 1				Profile Component 2		
	UA	N	A	M	UA	S	D
1					●		●
2				●	●		
3		●			●		
4		●					
5							
6							
7							
8							
9							
10							

N3/N4 Addition of sums of money.
M2 Using coins.
D1 Drawing mapping diagrams.

Handling the data – sample activities

- Draw mapping lines to link the sets of coins on the left to the sums of money on the right according to 'has a total value of' (**represent data**).

- Use coins to make five other sets which have total values of 5p, 6p, 7p, 8p and 9p (**using and applying**).

- See how many different sets you can make which have a total value of 7p (**using and applying**).

Interpreting the data – sample questions

- How many coins in each set on the left?
- What is the largest value on the right? What is the smallest?
- What is the total value of the top set of coins?
- Which set of coins sums to 6p, 7p,...?
- Which set of coins has the smallest, largest value?
- What is the total value of the top two sets of coins?
- How many 5p coins can you see? How many 2p, 1p coins?
- How much needs to be added to each set to make 10p?

Coin maps

   9p

   5p

   6p

   8p

   7p

Draw lines to link the sets of coins on the left to the sums of money on the right.

36 More or less

Recording with objects

Block graphs

Chance

Throwing a single dice numbered 1–6 and recording the outcome in terms of 'less than 3' or '3 or more' using counters.

Apparatus

Use a dice numbered 1–6 and a set of counters.

Activity

Throw the dice several times, and according to whether the outcome is 'less than 3' or '3 or more' record by placing a counter in the appropriate column, starting from the bottom upwards. Continue until a line of counters reaches the top.

LEVEL	Profile Component 1				Profile Component 2		
	UA	N	A	M	UA	S	D
1					●		●
2					●		●
3					●		●
4							
5							
6							
7							
8							
9							
10							

D1   Recording with real objects.
D2   Block graphs.
D3   Non-equally likely events of chance.

Handling the data – sample activities

- Pupils work in pairs, one choosing 'less than 3', the other choosing '3 or more'. The activity then becomes a competition to see who wins. Repeat the activity several times (**collect data**). Write about the results (**interpret data**).

- Draw a graph, using sticky squares or circles, to show the result of each throw (**represent data**).

- Make different pairs of labels to cover the 'less than 3' and '3 or more' on the sheet and repeat the activity.
  Examples of labels include:

  { 4 or more } and { less than 4 },

  { 5 or more } and { less than 5 },

  { 2 or 3 } and { 1, 4, 5 and 6 },

  (**using and applying**).

Interpreting the data – sample questions

- How many times did the dice show 'less than 3', '3 or more'?
- How many more times did the dice show '3 or more'?
- How many throws of the dice altogether?
- Which dice numbers are 'less than 3'?
- Which dice numbers are '3 or more'?
- What do you think would happen if you repeated the activity?

37 Down at the farm

Recording with objects

Tables

Counting the numbers of each animal on a farmyard. Recording the number of each with cubes and then listing them in a table.

LEVEL	Profile Component 1				Profile Component 2		
	UA	N	A	M	UA	S	D
1		●			●		●
2					●		
3					●		●
4							
5							
6							
7							
8							
9							
10							

N1 Counting.
D1 Recording with objects.
D3 Tables.

Handling the data – sample activities

- Colour the animals according to type.

- Record the number of each animal with cubes (**record data**).

- Draw a table listing the animals on the farm and the number of each (**process data**).
  Write about the table (**interpret data**).

- Draw your own farmyard with different animals. List the number of each type (**using and applying**).

Ducks ☐ ☐ ☐ ☐ ☐
Pigs ☐ ☐ ☐ ☐

Animal	Number
Ducks	6
Pigs	4

Interpreting the data – sample questions

- How many ducks, horses,... can you see?
- Of which animal are there two, seven,... in the picture?
- There are exactly three of some animals. Which ones?
- Of which animal are there most?
- How many more cats than dogs, cows than cats,...?
- How many fewer geese than chickens,...?
- How many humans can you see?
- Which creatures have two legs, four legs?

Down at the farm

38 Animals

Mapping diagrams

Block graphs

Consideration of sets containing 1, 2, 3, 4 or 5 animals. Completing mapping diagrams by joining the sets of animals with the numerals 1 to 5. Inventing similar mapping diagrams. Drawing block graphs to illustrate the number of animals in each set.

LEVEL	Profile Component 1				Profile Component 2		
	UA	N	A	M	UA	S	D
1					●		●
2					●		●
3					●		
4							
5							
6							
7							
8							
9							
10							

D1   Mapping diagrams.
D2   Block graphs.

Activity

Link the number of objects in each set with the numeral by an arrowed line.

Handling the data – sample activities

- Draw a graph to show the number of each type of animal (**represent data**).

- Invent your own mapping diagram with objects on the left and numerals on the right. Use real objects. Write about it (**using and applying**).

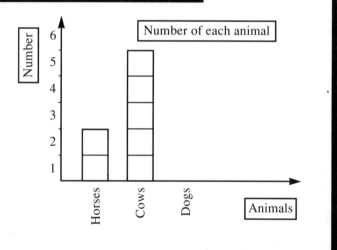

Interpreting the data – sample questions

- What are the different types of animal in the five sets?
- How many horses, cows,... are there?
- Which set has three animals, two animals, five animals,...?
- Which sets have more than two animals, less than five animals, between two and four animals?
- Are there more dogs than cats, fewer cows than horses,...?
- Which number is joined to the set of dogs?
- How many horses and cows are there altogether?
- How many of the animals are not cows?
- How many legs in each of the sets?

Animals

Draw lines to link the sets on the left to the numbers on the right.

39 Nine creatures

Sorting

Block graphs

Consideration of sets of creatures and the number in each set ranging from 1 to 9. Ordering the sets. Drawing block graphs to show the number in each set.

LEVEL	Profile Component 1				Profile Component 2		
	UA	N	A	M	UA	S	D
1		●					●
2							●
3							
4							
5							
6							
7							
8							
9							
10							

N1 Counting and ordering.
D1 Sorting ordering
D2 Block graphs.

Handling the data – sample activities

- Cut out the nine sets and arrange them in order smallest to largest (**process data**).

1	2	3	4	5	6	7	8	9
1 Giraffe	2 Goats	3 Cows						

- Stick the sets onto a strip of paper alongside the numerals (**represent data**).

- Draw a block graph to show the number in each set (**represent data**).

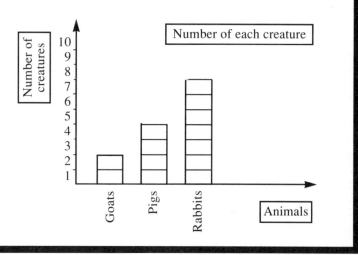

Interpreting the data – sample questions

- What type of creature is in A, B, C,...?
- How many goats, chickens,... are there?
- Which box contains three animals, five animals,...?
- Which set has the most?
- Which sets have more than five objects, fewer than four objects, between three and seven objects?
- How many animals are in the middle row, left-hand column?
- How many more cows than goats are there?
- Which creatures can fly?

Nine creatures

Write some sentences about these sets.

40 My family and friends

Mapping diagrams

Interpreting a mapping diagram illustrating the birthmonths of a child's family and friends. Drawing a similar mapping diagram.

LEVEL	Profile Component 1				Profile Component 2		
	UA	N	A	M	UA	S	D
1					●		●
2					●		
3					●		
4							
5							
6							
7							
8							
9							
10							

D1 Mapping diagrams.

Handling the data – sample activities

- **Collect data** on the birthmonths of your family and friends.

- Draw a mapping diagram to show their birthmonths. Write some sentences about the diagram (**using and applying; represent, interpret data**).

Interpreting the data – sample questions

- What month is Mum's, Grandad's,... birthday?
- Who has a birthday in June, July,...?
- Which month contains the birthday of two people?
- Which month has no birthdays?
- Which people were born in the winter, summer,...?
- Which people were born in the first half of the year, the second half?
- Does anybody have a birthday in the same month as you?

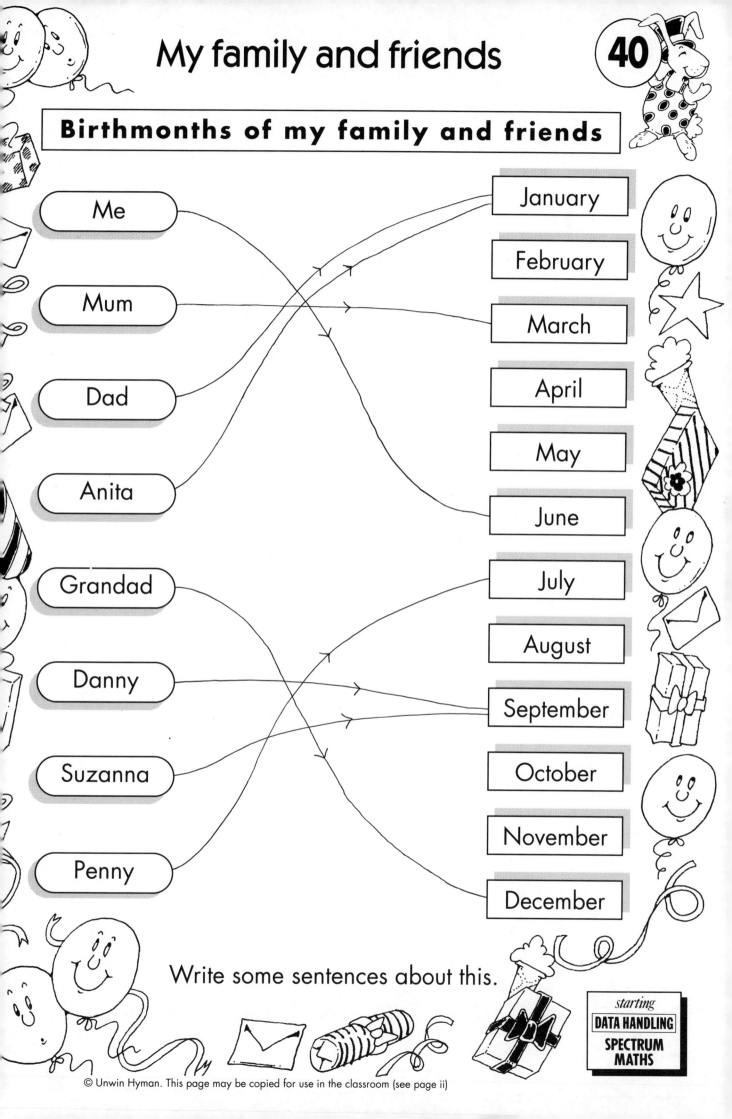

Spectrum Maths

The **Spectrum Maths Data Handling** series is a valuable addition to the other **Spectrum Maths** material. Namely:

Starting Games
More Games
Go Further with Games

Starting Investigations
More Investigations
Go Further with Investigations